CW00572719

www.booksbyboxer.com

Bee Three Publishing is an imprint of Books By Boxer
Published by
Books By Boxer, Leeds, LS13 4BS UK
Books by Boxer (EU), Dublin D02 P593 IRELAND
© Books By Boxer 2023
All Rights Reserved
**MADE IN MALTA**
ISBN: 9781915410245

MIX
Paper from
responsible sources
FSC® C022612

This book is produced from responsibly sourced paper to ensure forest management

# YOU MIGHT BE SHRINKING WITH OLD AGE,

BUT YOU WON'T BUMP YOUR HEAD ANYMORE!

"YOU KNOW YOU'RE GETTING OLD WHEN YOU STOOP TO TIE YOUR SHOELACES AND WONDER WHAT ELSE YOU COULD DO WHILE YOU'RE DOWN THERE."

- George Burns

You know you are getting old when you're cautioned to slow down by your doctor instead of by the police!

"YOU **DON'T STOP LAUGHING** WHEN YOU GROW OLD, YOU GROW OLD WHEN YOU STOP LAUGHING."

- George Bernard Shaw

YOU KNOW YOU'RE IN YOUR 50S WHEN YOUR HAIR GETS THINNER,

BUT YOU HAVE LESS HAIRCARE COSTS!

"The really frightening thing about middle age is that you know you'll grow out of it."

- Doris Day

# NOT SURE WHAT TO HAVE FOR DINNER?

SOON YOU'LL BE ABLE TO ASK THE CARE HOME CHEF!

# GOALS FOR THE YEAR:

GET OUT OF THE ARMCHAIR IN ONE TRY ☐

DON'T MISPLACE YOUR TEETH FOR A WHOLE WEEK ☐

DON'T SAY "BACK IN MY DAY" ☐

# THE OLDER YOU GET, THE CLOSER

## TO A TOILET YOU NEED TO BE.

"I don't feel old. I don't feel anything until noon. Then it's time for my nap."

- Bob Hope

YOU KNOW
YOU'RE IN YOUR
50s WHEN
YOU HAVE
AN EARLIER
BEDTIME...

BUT YOUR JOINTS STILL ACHE.

"BIRTHDAYS ARE GOOD FOR YOU. STATISTICS SHOW THAT THE PEOPLE WHO HAVE THE MOST LIVE THE LONGEST."

- Unknown

Life's all about a trade off...your memory is shorter but your complaining has gotten longer!

"GROWING OLD IS MANDATORY, BUT **GROWING UP IS OPTIONAL.**"

- Walt Disney

# MID-LIFE CRISIS CHECKLIST:

- [ ] BUY A NEW CAR

- [ ] DRASTIC COSMETIC SURGERY

- [ ] GET A NEW TATTOO – OR 3...

- [ ] DYE YOUR HAIR PINK

- [ ] DATE SOMEONE HALF YOUR AGE

"Today is the oldest you have been and the youngest you'll ever be again."

- Eleanor Roosevelt

# AT 50, YOU HAVE GOTTEN YOUR HEAD TOGETHER, BUT YOUR BODY HAS STARTED TO FALL APART!

"Old age is not so bad when you consider the alternative."

- Maurice Chevalier

# HERE'S TO YOUR TO YOUR INEVITABLE

JOINT PAIN!

"EVENTUALLY YOU WILL REACH A POINT WHEN YOU **STOP LYING ABOUT YOUR AGE** AND **START BRAGGING ABOUT IT.**"

- Will Rogers

# YOUTH IS WASTED

## ON THE YOUNG!

"I DON'T LET MY AGE DEFINE ME BUT THE SIDE-EFFECTS ARE GETTING HARDER TO IGNORE."

- Unknown

You know you're getting old when someone phones after 9pm, and asks 'sorry, did I wake you?'

# THINGS YOUR HEART OFFICIALLY CAN'T HANDLE

**HORROR FILMS** ☐

**A COLD SPRITE** ☐

**FAST MUSIC** ☐

**ROLLERCOASTERS** ☐

# 'AGE' IS A NUMBER.

'OLD' IS IN YOUR HEAD!

"Age is an issue of mind over matter. If you don't mind, it doesn't matter."

- Mark Twain

# HAVE YOU EVER LEFT A CONCERT EARLY TO 'BEAT THE RUSH'?

YEP. YOU'RE OLD.

"Age is not a particularly interesting subject. Anyone can get old. All you have to do is live long enough."

- Groucho Marx

YOUR TATTOOS MIGHT BE FADING,

BUT YOUR WRINKLES WILL COVER THEM!

"DON'T LET AGING GET YOU DOWN. IT'S TOO HARD TO GET BACK UP."

- John Wagner

## THINGS PEOPLE MIGHT SAY TO YOU ON YOUR BIRTHDAY:

- [ ] YOU'RE HOW OLD?!

- [ ] AGE IS JUST A NUMBER

- [ ] YOU'RE ONLY AS YOUNG AS YOU FEEL

- [ ] I'VE ALREADY ALERTED THE FIRE DEPARTMENT, SO GO AHEAD AND LIGHT THE CANDLES ON YOUR CAKE

"YOU KNOW YOU
ARE GETTING
OLD WHEN
EVERYTHING
EITHER DRIES UP
OR LEAKS."

- Will Rogers

The trick to staying young as you get older is finding an age you really like, and sticking with it!

"AGE IS JUST A
NUMBER. IT'S TOTALLY
IRRELEVANT UNLESS,
OF COURSE, YOU
HAPPEN TO BE A
BOTTLE OF WINE."

- Joan Collins

YOU KNOW YOU'RE IN YOUR 50s WHEN IT HAS STARTED TO TAKE TWICE AS LONG...

TO LOOK HALF AS GOOD!

"Wisdom doesn't necessarily come with age. Sometimes age just shows up all by itself."

- Tom Wilson

# YOU ARE ONLY YOUNG ONCE,

BUT YOU CAN STAY IMMATURE INDEFINITELY!

"You know you're getting old when the candles cost more than the cake."

- Bob Hope

Maybe it's time to light your candles outside now! You know, for health and safety reasons.

# WAYS TO LIE ABOUT YOUR AGE:

I'M 21 PLUS VAT ☐

NEVER ASK A LADY HER AGE! ☐

IT'S A TRADE SECRET... ☐

SORRY, CAN YOU REPEAT THAT? ☐

OLDER THAN I'VE EVER BEEN
(BEFORE I FORGOT) ☐

SAME AS MY IQ SCORE ☐

# YOU KNOW YOU'RE GETTING OLD

WHEN YOU HEAR YOUR FAVORITE SONGS IN AN ELEVATOR.

"AS YOU GET OLDER THREE THINGS HAPPEN. THE FIRST IS YOUR MEMORY GOES, AND I CAN'T REMEMBER THE OTHER TWO."

- Norman Wisdom

# LIFE IS JUST BIRTHDAYS,

WITH A CONSTANT SIDE EFFECT OF AGING!

# "There is still no cure for the common birthday."

- John Glenn

**YOUR EYESIGHT MIGHT BE GETTING WORSE,** BUT AT LEAST IT PROTECTS YOU FROM YOUR REFLECTION IN THE MIRROR!

"Forty is the old age of youth; fifty the youth of old age."

- Victor Hugo

# SIGNS YOU'RE GETTING OLDER:

☐ 6AM IS WHEN YOU GET UP NOT GET IN

☐ HAIR SEEMS TO SPROUTING UP EVERYWHERE IT'S NOT SUPPOSED TO!

☐ YOU WAKE UP STIFF

☐ COMPLAIN THAT THE TV WAS BETTER BACK IN YOUR DAY

☐ CAR INSURANCE IS CHEAPER THAN LIFE INSURANCE

"**OLD AGE**
COMES AT
A BAD TIME."

- San Banducci

You know you're 50 when you've been there and done that, but don't remember what that was.

"LIFE IS LIKE A ROLL OF TOILET PAPER. THE CLOSER YOU GET TO THE END, THE FASTER IT GOES."

- Unknown

# YOUR FAVORITE PLANS

ARE THE CANCELED ONES!

# "I'm at an age when my back goes out more than I do."

- Phyllis Diller

# YOU KNOW YOU'RE GETTING OLD,

WHEN YOU'RE ENTERING YOUR DATE OF BIRTH ONLINE AND HAVE TO SCROLL DOWN!

"Old people shouldn't eat health foods. They need all the preservatives they can get."

- Robert Orben

# DON'T
# WORRY,

YOU DON'T LOOK A DAY OVER 49!

# YOU KNOW YOU'RE OLD WHEN YOU'RE EXCITED FOR:

- NEW VITAMINS ☐
- NEW VACUUM CLEANER ☐
- SMELLING THE FRESH WASHING ☐
- HAPPY HOUR – (NAPTIME) ☐
- RUSHING HOME JUST TO CHILL ON THE COUCH ☐

You've been alive for 18,262 days now!

"TO ME, OLD AGE
IS ALWAYS 15 YEARS
OLDER THAN I AM."

- Bernard M. Baruch

YOU KNOW YOU'RE IN YOR 50s WHEN YOUR YOUR KNEES BUCKLE,

BUT YOUR BELT WONT!

# "Don't just count your years, make your years count."

- George Meredith

YOU KNOW YOU'RE IN YOUR 50s WHEN IT FEELS LIKE THE MORNING AFTER, BUT THERE WAS NO NIGHT BEFORE!

# "Live your life and forget your age."

- Norman Vincent Peale

# ALTERNATIVE WAYS TO SAY YOU'RE OLD:

- [ ] POST-ADOLESCENT

- [ ] VINTAGE

- [ ] WELL MATURED

- [ ] COFFIN DODGER

- [ ] ANTIQUE

"OLD AGE IS LIKE A PLANE FLYING THROUGH A STORM. ONCE YOU ARE ABOARD THERE IS NOTHING YOU CAN DO ABOUT IT."

- Golda Meir

# The gleam in your eye is from the sun hitting your bifocals!

"THE SECRET OF STAYING YOUNG IS TO **LIVE HONESTLY**, EAT SLOWLY, AND **LIE ABOUT YOUR AGE**."

- Lucille Ball

# DON'T BE SCARED OF SCARED OF WRINKLES,

THEY DON'T HURT!

# "It's important to have a twinkle in your wrinkle."

- Unknown

# GOOD NEWS: PEOPLE CAN LOOK BETTER AS THEY AGE.

BAD NEWS: A LOT OF TIMES, PEOPLE DON'T.

"You're not as young as you used to be. But you're not as old as you're going to be."

- Irish Saying

# TIME IS A GREAT HEALER

(BUT A LOUSY BEAUTICIAN!)

# NOISES MADE GETTING OUT OF BED:

OOOOH ☐

UNGH ☐

OH GOD ☐

GRRRRR ☐

BIG PUSH ☐

ARGH ☐

JESUS CHRIST! ☐

Your midlife crisis has officially started... you just don't need to pretend it hasn't any more!

"YOU'VE HEARD OF THE THREE AGES OF MAN: YOUTH, MIDDLE AGE, AND **YOU'RE LOOKING WONDERFUL**."

- Cardinal Spellman

# THE OLDER YOU GET, THE QUICKER

YOU REVERT BACK TO MUSHY FOODS!

**"Age is a number and mine is unlisted."**

- Unknown

# YOU FINALLY GET YOUR HEAD TOGETHER

AND YOUR BODY STARTS FALLING APART!

"You know you've aged when you read events you lived in a history book."

- Will Ferrell

## WAYS TO DISGUISE YOUR WRINKLES:

- ☐ HALLOWEEN MASK

- ☐ PAPER BAG

- ☐ STICKY TAPE

- ☐ SEALANT

- ☐ FAKE HAIR

"INSIDE EVERY OLDER PERSON IS A YOUNGER PERSON — WONDERING WHAT THE HELL HAPPENED."

- Jennifer Yane

You're officially 'You look good for your age' years old!

"THE WAY I SEE IT, YOU SHOULD **LIVE EVERY DAY LIKE IT'S YOUR BIRTHDAY.**"

- Paris Hilton

# HOW MANY TIMES DOES IT TAKE TO GET UP...

## FROM THE COUCH?

"I intend to live forever — so far, so good!"

- Stephen Wright

# HAPPY HOUR USED TO BE ABOUT MUSIC AND COCKTAILS...

NOW IT'S JUST A NAP!

"All the world is birthday cake, so take a piece, but not too much."

- George Harrison

# YOU KNOW YOU'RE OLD

WHEN YOU AND YOUR TEETH DON'T SLEEP TOGETHER!

# REASONS TO EMBRACE YOUR AGE:

EACH WRINKLE IS A MEDAL ☐

YOUR TEETH CAN BE TAKEN OUT TO WASH ☐

CATERPILLARS? BROWS? WHO KNOWS! ☐

CHEAPER BUS FARES ☐

NEED NO EXCUSES TO STAY IN ☐

GET OFFERED TO GO FIRST IN QUEUES ☐

You know you're old when you blow out your candles and your teeth fall out!

"**IT IS NEVER TOO LATE** TO BE WHAT YOU MIGHT HAVE BEEN."

- George Eliot

# LAUGHING IS LIKE JOGGING

## ON THE INSIDE!

"And in the end, it's not the years in your life that count. It's the life in your years."

- Abraham Lincoln

**YOU KNOW YOU'RE IN YOUR 50S WHEN YOUR FEET NO LONGER LOOK NICE, BUT YOU'RE THE RIGHT AGE TO ROCK SOCKS AND SANDALS!**

# "At 50, everyone has the face he deserves."

- George Orwell

You know you're old when your slippers become your outdoor shoes.